A LOOK AT LIFE SCIENCE

WHAT ARE PROTISTS?

BY KATE MIKOLEY

Gareth Stevens PUBLISHING

CRASHCOURSE

Please visit our website, www.garethstevens.com. For a free color catalog of all our high-quality books, call toll free 1-800-542-2595 or fax 1-877-542-2596.

Cataloging-in-Publication Data

Names: Mikoley, Kate.
Title: What are protists? / Kate Mikoley.
Description: New York : Gareth Stevens Publishing, 2020. | Series: A look at life science | Includes glossary and index.
Identifiers: ISBN 9781538248638(pbk.) | ISBN 9781538248652 (library bound) | ISBN 9781538248645 (6 pack)
Subjects: LCSH: Protista--Juvenile literature.
Classification: LCC QR74.5 M63 2020 | DDC 579--dc23

First Edition

Published in 2020 by
Gareth Stevens Publishing
111 East 14th Street, Suite 349
New York, NY 10003

Designer: Reann Nye
Editor: Kate Mikoley

Photo credits: Series art MriMan/Shutterstock.com; cover, pp. 1, 30 (middle) Lebendkulturen.de/Shutterstock.com; p. 5 Calvvin/Shutterstock.com; p. 7 corbac40/Shutterstock.com; pp. 9, 30 (bottom) Simia Attentive/Shutterstock.com; p. 11 Viktoriia Hnatiuk/Shutterstock.com; p. 13 Adwo/Shutterstock.com; p. 15 Paul Whitted/Shutterstock.com; p. 17 STEVE GSCHMEISSNER/SCIENCE PHOTO LIBRARY/Science Photo Library/Getty Images Plus/Getty Images; p. 19 Roland Birke/Photolibrary/Getty Images Plus/Getty Images; p. 21 Amir Ridhwan/Shutterstock.com; p. 23 Khalit Chaush-ogly/Shutterstock.com; p. 25 Matt Meadows/Photolibrary/Getty Images Plus/Getty Images; p. 27 Gorodenkoff/Shutterstock.com; p. 29 Henri Koskinen/Shutterstock.com; p. 30 (top) C N Elliott/Shutterstock.com.

Printed in the United States of America

CPSIA compliance information: Batch #CW20GS: For further information contact Gareth Stevens, New York, New York at 1-800-542-2595.

CONTENTS

Words in the glossary appear in **bold** type the first time they are used in the text.

LITTLE LIFE FORMS

The world is full of living things called organisms. You likely see organisms such as plants and animals every day. However, some living things aren't so easy to spot. A protist is a kind of tiny organism usually made up of one cell.

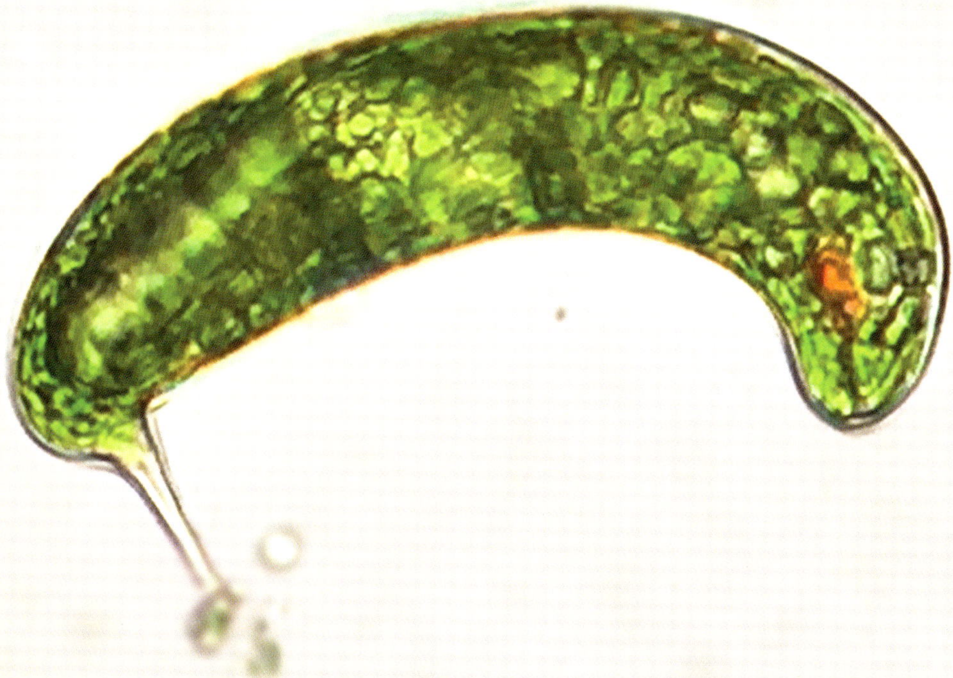

MAKE THE GRADE

When an organism is made up of only one cell, it's called unicellular. Most, but not all, protists are unicellular.

Protists are eukaryotes. Eukaryotes are organisms that have a **membrane** around the **nucleus**, making it easy to see. Animals, plants, and **fungi** are also examples of eukaryotes. However, protists often have different features than these other organisms.

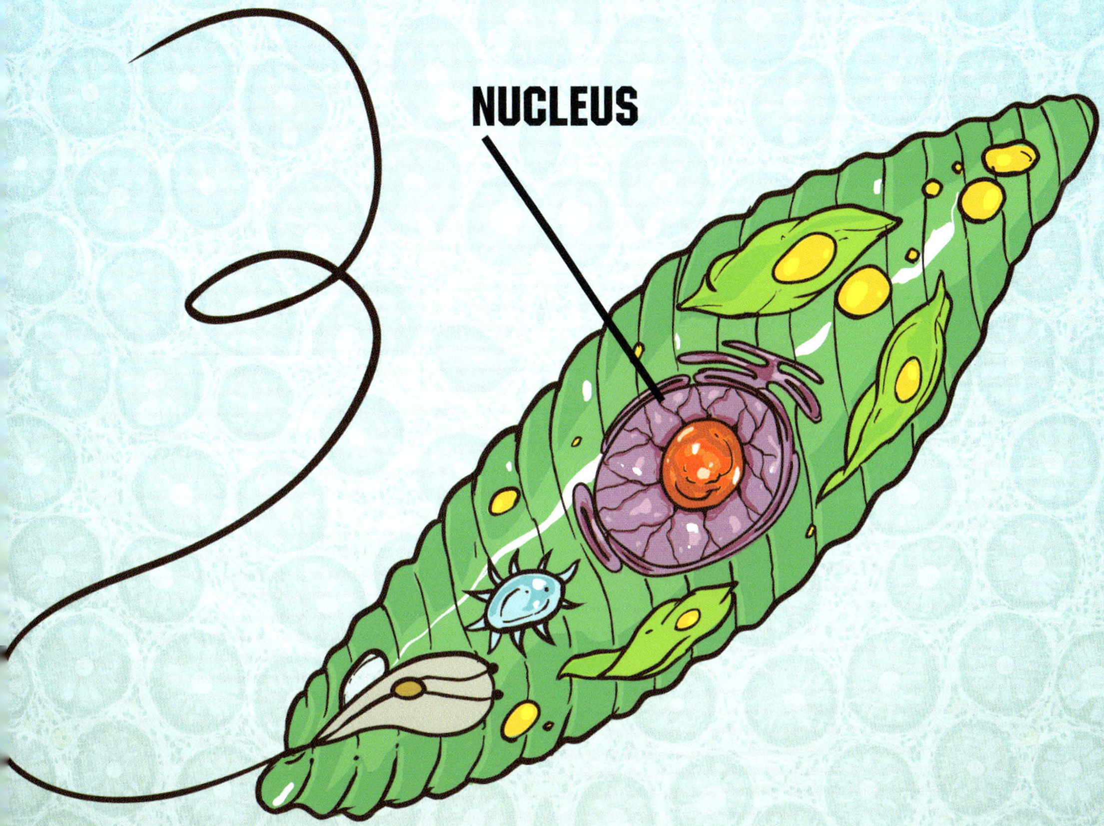

MAKE THE GRADE

The word "protist" is commonly used to mean any eukaryote that is not a plant, animal, or fungus.

A RANGE OF PROTISTS

There are thousands of species, or kinds, of protists. From species to species, these organisms can be very different from one another. Some kinds of protists move around and act sort of like animals. Other kinds act more like plants or fungi.

MAKE THE GRADE

Some protists are solitary, meaning they live alone. Others join together and make up groups called colonies.

Many kinds of protists live in water. Others live on land, but still need water to survive. These protists are commonly found in **damp** areas. Some protists even live inside animals! These are called parasites.

MAKE THE GRADE

Lots of protists are so small that you need a special tool called a microscope to see them.

ALL ABOUT ALGAE

If you've ever swum in an ocean or lake, you're likely familiar with at least one kind of protist—even if you don't know it! Algae are protists that commonly live in water. They often look and act like plants.

MAKE THE GRADE

Protists that act like plants can make their own food through **photosynthesis**.

Algae that grow in the ocean are commonly called seaweed. A kind of seaweed called kelp is an example of a protist with many cells. While most protists are very small, some kinds of kelp can be more than 200 feet (61 m) long!

MAKE THE GRADE

Giant kelp is the largest protist known about in the world today.

ACTING LIKE ANIMALS

Protozoans are a kind of protist that sometimes act like animals. Some types are able to move from place to place and get **nutrients** by feeding on other organisms. Many protozoans eat bacteria and other protists. Some eat small animals!

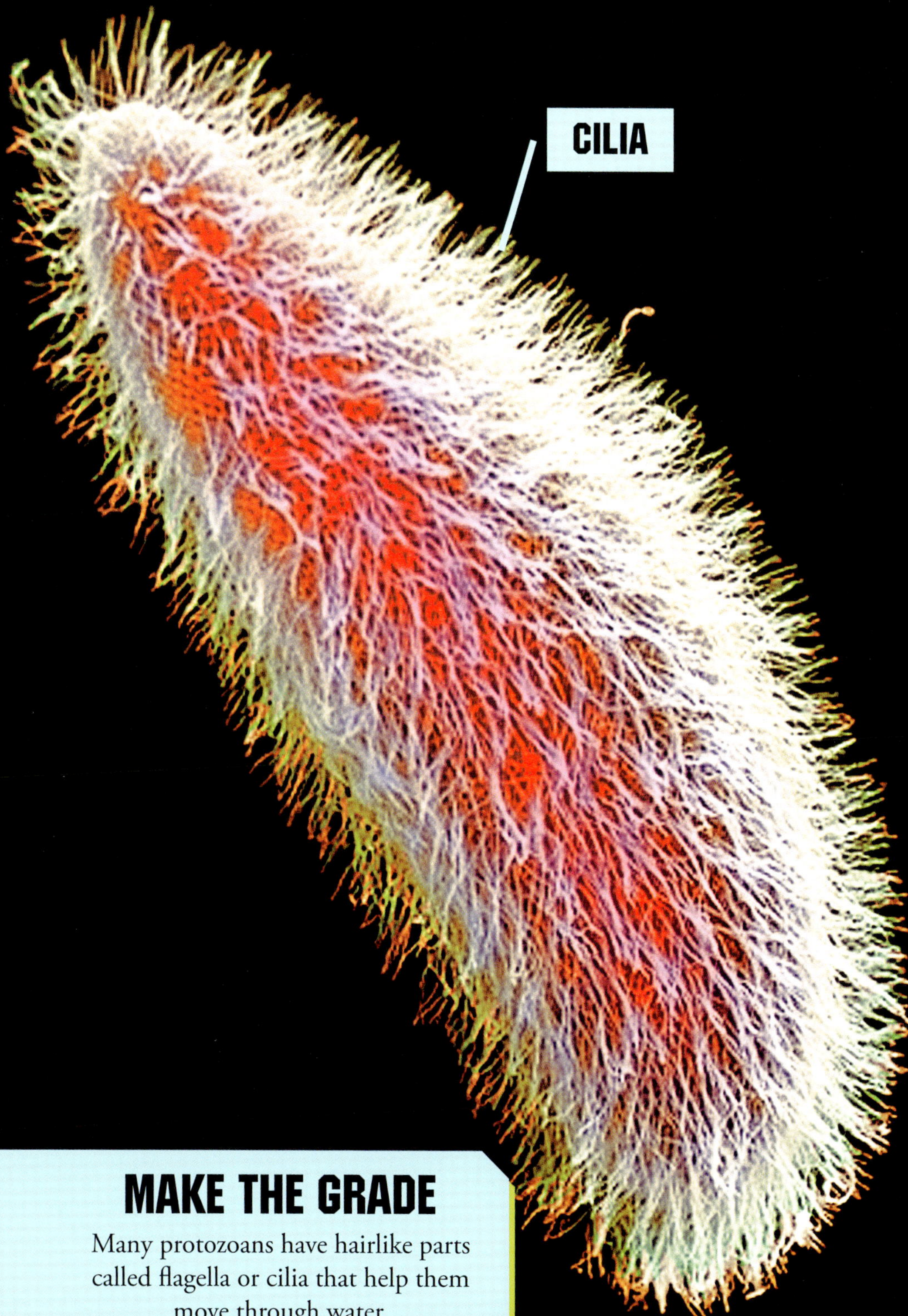

MAKE THE GRADE

Many protozoans have hairlike parts called flagella or cilia that help them move through water.

Amoebas are a type of protozoan. They use parts called pseudopodia to move around. These are parts of the cell that are formed and drawn out from the body when needed. They help the amoeba hold on to a surface and move.

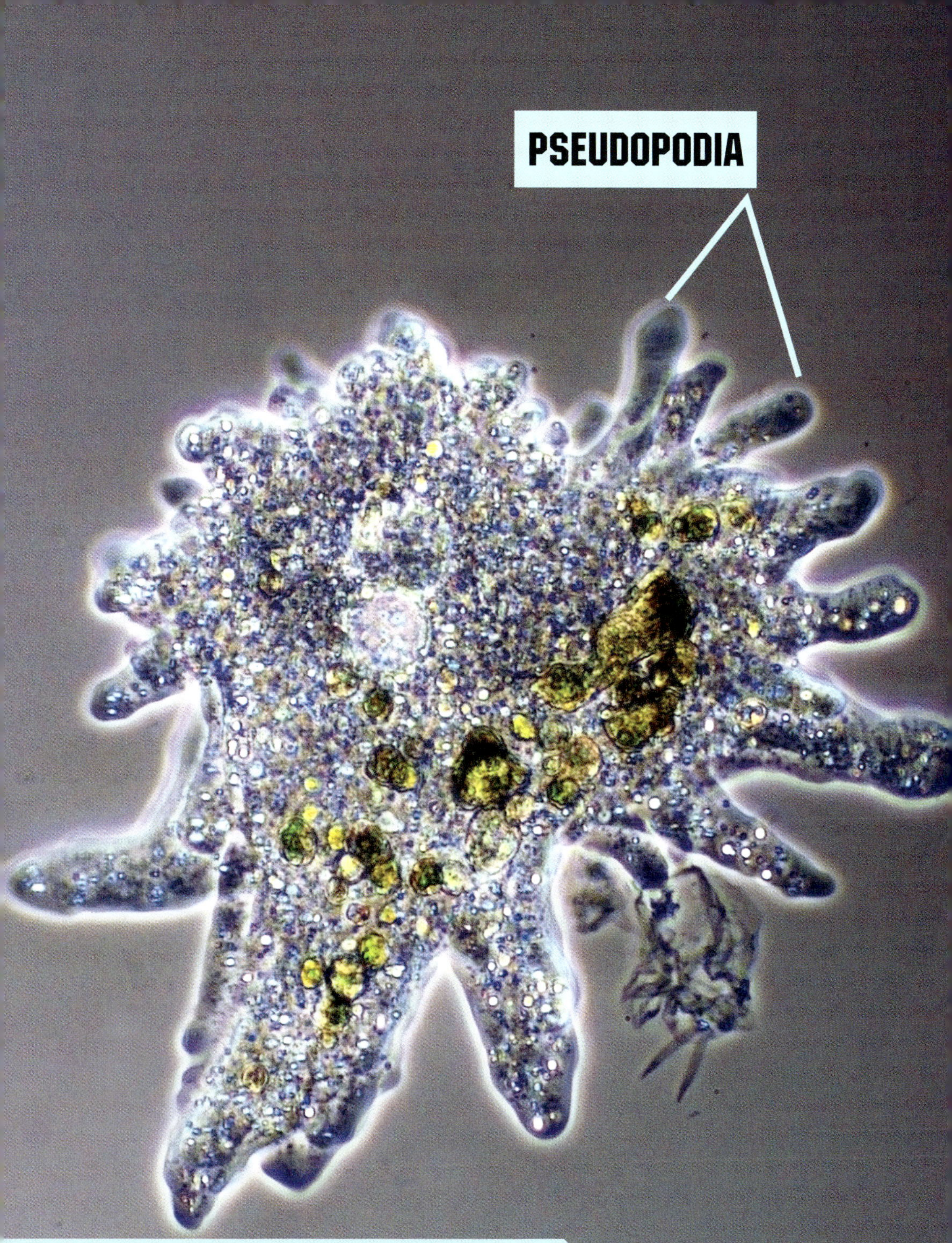

MAKE THE GRADE

The word "pseudopodia" comes from the Greek language. It means "false feet."

Plasmodium is a kind of protozoan that is a parasite. It can **infect** the red blood cells of many kinds of animals. It can cause an illness called malaria. In humans, malaria can cause **fevers**, chills, and other serious problems.

MAKE THE GRADE

Plasmodium can be passed to animals through the bite of a female *Anopheles* mosquito.

SLIMY PROTISTS

Slime molds are a kind of protist that were once thought to be fungi. They do share some features with fungi. For example, they sometimes make spores. Slime molds and fungi both use spores to **reproduce**.

MAKE THE GRADE

Some slime molds live on dead plant matter. Many kinds of fungi also do this.

In some ways, slime molds also act like animals. They can move around! They may move as single cells. However, sometimes many of the cells come together, making a **layer** that can move around the floor of the forest!

MAKE THE GRADE

Slime molds aren't necessarily speedy. One kind, *Physarum polycephalum*, only reaches about 0.04 inch (1 mm) per hour.

PRETTY COOL PROTISTS

Many protists are very helpful. For example, algae produce **oxygen** during photosynthesis. Scientists think algae likely give us about half the oxygen in the world. Protists also provide food for many other organisms in the world.

MAKE THE GRADE

Scientists often study protists to learn more about cells. They have also been used in studies to learn how certain illnesses can be treated.

Protists are commonly sorted by whether they act like plants, animals, or fungi. However, it's important to remember that they're not any of those organisms. They are their own group of very **diverse** and special living things!

MAKE THE GRADE

Protists can be so different from one another that the **kingdom** is sometimes called the "junk drawer kingdom."

LIVING LIKE A PROTIST

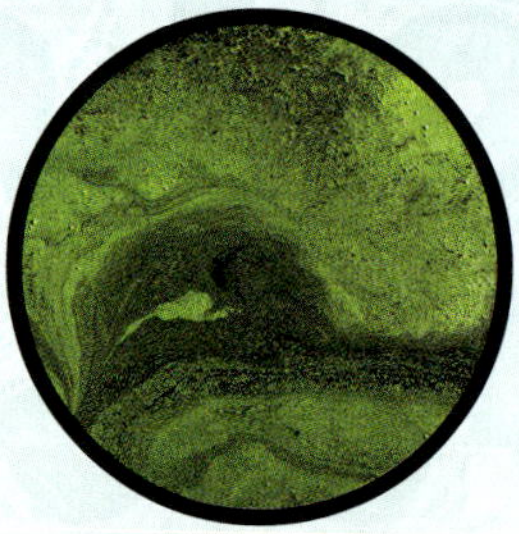

ALGAE and plants often make their own food through photosynthesis.

PROTOZOANS, SLIME MOLDS, and animals often move around and eat other organisms.

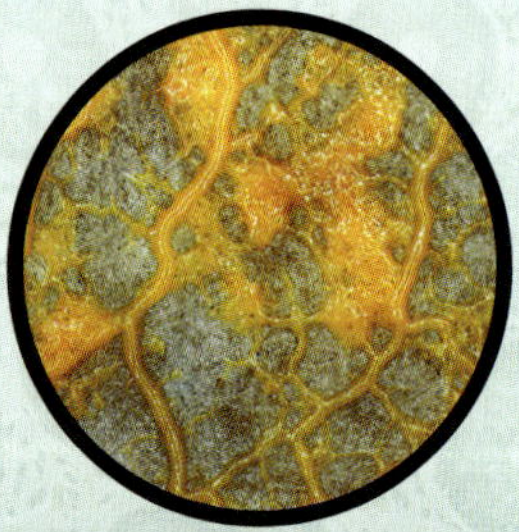

SLIME MOLDS and fungi often reproduce using spores.

GLOSSARY

damp: somewhat wet

diverse: differing from each other

fever: a body temperature higher than normal or healthy

fungi: living things that are somewhat like plants, but don't make their own food, have leaves, or have a green color

infect: to spread something harmful

kingdom: a major group into which organisms can be sorted

layer: one thickness of something lying over or under another

membrane: a soft, thin layer of living matter

nucleus: the central part of a eukaryotic cell

nutrient: something a living thing needs to grow and stay alive

oxygen: a colorless, odorless gas that many animals, including people, need to breathe

photosynthesis: the process by which green plants and some protists use light to turn water and carbon dioxide into food

reproduce: when an organism creates another creature just like itself

FOR MORE INFORMATION

BOOKS

Arbuthnott, Gill. *Your Guide to Life on Earth*. New York, NY: Crabtree Publishing Company, 2016.

Spilsbury, Louise and Richard. *Microorganisms*. Chicago, IL: Heinemann Library, 2014.

WEBSITES

Biology for Kids: Protists
www.ducksters.com/science/biology/protists.php
Find out even more about protists and take a quiz about them here.

The Blob: Slime Molds
herbarium.usu.edu/fun-with-fungi/slime-molds
Read up on more information about slime molds on this website.

Publisher's note to educators and parents: Our editors have carefully reviewed these websites to ensure that they are suitable for students. Many websites change frequently, however, and we cannot guarantee that a site's future contents will continue to meet our high standards of quality and educational value. Be advised that students should be closely supervised whenever they access the internet.

INDEX